Whatever Is True

A Christian View of
Anxiety

D0584615

William Woodington

NORTHWESTERN PUBLISHING HOUSE
Milwaukee, Wisconsin

Northwestern Publishing House
N16W23379 Stone Ridge Dr., Waukesha, WI 53188
www.nph.net
© 2020 Northwestern Publishing House
Published 2020
Printed in the United States of America
ISBN 978-0-8100-3001-5

21 22 23 24 25 26 27 28 29   10 9 8 7 6 5 4 3 2

Contents

Preface

So where do I begin? So many of these types of books begin with a personal account of how the individual first became affected by panic and anxiety. But if I start that way, what good would that do for you? To show you that I myself have been affected as you have? To convince you I know what you have been through? To better align myself with you? If nothing else, it would probably have the adverse effect intended—getting you to focus on fear—and that is not why I am writing this book.

No, I prefer to take a different approach. It doesn't really matter how you got here. It doesn't really matter in what situations, what stage of life, or how anxiety and panic came to affect you. The point is, you have had this come into your life and you are looking for answers.

And who am I to give you those answers? I am not a doctor in the field of psychology nor an expert in some new breakthrough psychological theory in the field of anxiety disorders. I am not here to tell you about some new drug that cures all your ills. No, I am a Christian, and I have much to share. I believe personal experience can teach much, but the Holy Spirit teaches us best as he speaks to us through God's Word.

If you're reading this book, you may have read many self-help books related to this topic. I've read many and have been influenced by several. Claire Weekes' *Hope and Help for Your Nerves* had a profound impact on me. She had it right. Her theory of Facing, Accepting, Floating, and Letting Time Pass makes sense. Weekes just didn't realize where her insight came from. She didn't realize her theory had connections to Bible teachings.

For me, I couldn't deviate from the teachings in the Bible. No matter how painful my situation was, any help that was to come my way had to be consistent with the Word of God. "What good is it for a man to gain the whole world and yet forfeit his soul?" (Mark 8:36). What good would it be for me to be free of panic if I turned away from God during times he taught and disciplined me? What would I have gained if I learned to trust in me and not in him? Don't get me wrong, it wasn't that I couldn't use recommendations from self-help books, but those books had to be an earthly way of implementing what God was telling me through his Word. And, as I said, I found this in Weekes' teachings to a great degree. But something was missing.

Weekes didn't have the full story. Her words didn't have the true power that could free me. Why? Because every self-help book describes it this way: You have the ability to get out of this mess on your own. Why else do they call these books "self-help"? What a burden! If I am my only hope, look at the mess I create for myself. If I am the only way out, where does my strength come from? Me? I am living proof that weakness lies within me. The so-called experts have stumbled over the stumbling stone—trusting in themselves instead of God. "They kept pursuing it not by faith, but as if it comes by works. They stumbled over the stumbling stone. Just as it is written: "Look, I am putting a stone in Zion over which they will stumble and a rock over which they will fall. The one who believes in him will not be put to shame" (Romans 9:32,33). And who is this stumbling stone? Jesus Christ.

So much of our world today glorifies those who can help themselves. We hear that the people who have pulled themselves up by the bootstraps in the direst of situations makes them what they are today. What a shame. If only they knew who truly pulled them up. I recently read Lance Armstrong's book, *It's Not About the Bike.* After reading it, I sent an email to Armstrong's foundation telling him how his book had missed an opportunity. The book could have been a great witness to what God had done for him. Instead, it was a bootstraps book. Armstrong was at the brink of death with testicular cancer. The book tells of his struggles and his inner strength, which led to his cure. He trusted in himself instead of God—the stumbling stone again.

Martin Luther wrote in his Small Catechism, "I believe that I cannot by my own thinking or choosing believe in Jesus Christ, my Lord, nor come to him." A person cannot come to faith on his own. And the same can be said about anxiety—you cannot free yourself from anxiety with your own might or strength. Faith comes from God . . . and so does peace. The Holy Spirit moved the apostle Paul to capture so well about being saved and having faith: "This is not from yourselves, it is the gift of God—not by works, so that no one can boast" (Ephesians 2:8,9).

I want to share the truth with you. The Bible says, "Finally, brothers, whatever is true, whatever is honorable, whatever is right, whatever is pure, whatever is lovely, whatever is commendable, if anything is excellent, and if anything is praiseworthy, think about these things" (Philippians 4:8). What is truth? What should you be thinking about? Truth is found only in God's Word. And, believe it or not, his Word applies to anxiety. His Word will set you free. Not only in this life but, more important, in the life to come.

So this book is more about faith in God and what he has revealed to us in his Word. It's more about what he has done, and will do, for you and me in this life and the life beyond. It is framed in the context of dealing with anxiety and panic. That's the way God chose to discipline me to bring me closer to him.

ONE

Sin

"Certainly, I was guilty when I was born.
I was sinful when my mother conceived me."

Psalm 51:5

Why do we suffer in this world? Why has anxiety come into our lives? The world, including the medical profession, will give numerous answers. They will have you explore your family genes, revisit your childhood, examine past experiences, follow a path back to your failures—always looking back. We can't totally discount the past. Your genes and past experiences have had a great impact on who you are today. But if these genes and past experiences are less than perfect, how come? What's the true reason behind our suffering?

I can remember in my childhood thinking what a beautiful place the world is. I can remember the joy in my inner being when I chased butterflies, fished in a nearby creek, and played baseball with neighborhood boys. I had few troubles and cares to think about. Heavy responsibilities weren't a heavy weight in my life. My parents, teachers, and other adults shouldered my burdens. But before long, these burdens fell on me. I soon realized the world is not a perfect place, and I'm not a perfect person.

In junior high, a bully had it in for me. Every day he sought me out for a fight. I dreaded that time of day when I knew we'd have our encounter. My mental state became a problem. At home after school, I'd worry about this. I'd even say to myself, "You don't have any problems." Push away the problems. Avoid them at all cost. That's what I tried to convince myself would help. But that was a lie—I did have problems. Eventually I confronted the bully, but nothing really happened. What I didn't realize was that God rescued me. Soon other troubles arose; other worries made their way into my mind. I didn't know it then, but in this life, I would always have problems. Jesus promises this to us: "In this world you are going to have trouble" (John 16:33). With more troubles, more worries, and more problems, I began to see the world in a different light.

Where were those happy days? I didn't want to worry, but I did. I didn't want to be scared of things, but I was. The apostle Paul helps to answer why I had the problems: "I fail to do the good I want to do. Instead, the evil I do not want to do, that is what I keep doing. Now if I do what I do not want to do, it is no longer I who am doing it, but it is sin living in me" (Romans 7:19,20).

There lies the answer to the true reason behind our suffering. It's sin living in us.

And why does sin live in us? Because people disobeyed God. It started with our ancestors Adam and Eve. God said, "You shall not eat from it. You shall not touch it, or else you will die" (Genesis 3:3). And what did they do? "When the woman saw that the tree was good for food, and that it was appealing to the eyes, and that the tree was desirable to make one wise, she took some of its fruit and ate. She gave some also to her husband, who was with her, and he ate it" (Genesis 3:6). And how did God respond? To Eve he said, "I will greatly increase your pain in childbearing. With painful labor you will give birth to children" (Genesis 3:16). To Adam he said, "The soil is cursed on account of you. You will eat from it with painful labor all the days of your life. Thorns and thistles will spring up from the ground for you, but you will eat the crops of the field. By the sweat of your face you will eat bread until you return to the soil, for out of it you were taken. For you are dust, and to dust you shall return" (Genesis 3:17-19).

So my troubles are due to Adam and Eve? Yes . . . and also due to you. Sin lived in them, and it lives in you. Without sin, you would have no troubles, no problems, no worries, and no anxiety. Humankind's relationship with God changed in the Garden of Eden. Disobedience brought sin. Disobedience brought death. Disobedience destroyed humankind's unity with God in thoughts, words, and actions.

Paul sums up the events of Genesis chapter 3 in this way: "Just as sin entered the world through one man and death through sin, so also death spread to all people because all sinned" (Romans 5:12). Psalm 53 states the sad thing God sees: "God looks down from heaven on all the children of Adam to see if there is anyone who understands, anyone who seeks God. Every single one has turned back. Altogether they have become rotten. There is no one who does good. There is not even one" (verses 2,3). Not you, not me. No one is excluded, as God clearly says, "All have sinned and fall short of the glory of God" (Romans 3:23).

What caused Adam and Eve to sin? Go to Genesis 3:13. Eve states, "The serpent deceived me, and I ate." Who is this serpent, this deceiver? It's our true enemy—the devil, Satan.

Do you think your struggle is against anxiety? No, not even close. Anxiety is not your enemy. In fact, as we'll later see, if you never conquer anxiety, you will have lost nothing. The Bible describes your true struggle, and it's not against anxiety: "Our struggle is not against flesh and blood, but against the rulers, against the authorities, against the world rulers of this darkness, against the spiritual forces of evil in the heavenly places" (Ephesians 6:12). Your struggle is against the one who fights to take you away from God, the one who tries to rob you of your faith in God, the one who attempts to take you from your heavenly home. Your struggle is against spiritual forces of evil—Satan and his demon army. They may use anxiety to get you to trust in yourself. If you become anxiety-free and believe it is due to your own doing, the devil and his minions have won a substantial victory. That is why I previously said that I couldn't deviate from the Bible's teachings. God would be my way out, not me. Heaven is my goal, not freedom from anxiety.

Earlier in this book, Philippians 4:8 told us what should occupy our thoughts (those things that are true, honorable, right, pure, lovely, etc.). But our thoughts don't always rest upon such things. So much of what we think about, and believe, is just not true! Who manipulates those thoughts? Who leads us to believe those lies? Who plays on our sinful nature? It's the same one who slithered up to the side of Adam and Eve and deceived them.

The apostle John writes, "He was a murderer from the beginning and did not remain standing in the truth, because there is no truth in him. Whenever he lies, he speaks from what is his, because he is a liar and the father of lying" (John 8:44). Who is this father of lying? Satan. Your enemy from the first day of your life. Your enemy until the day you die. The one who loves to see you afraid. "Your adversary, the Devil, prowls around like a roaring lion, looking for someone to devour. Resist him by being firm in the faith. You know that the same kinds of sufferings are being laid on your brotherhood all over the world" (1 Peter 5:8,9).

The nonbeliever discounts the devil as some mythical creature to be believed in by the weak and timid. That's a lie. Where do you think that lie comes from? It's from the devil who wants you to discount him as your powerful enemy. For those who believe the lie, he has them right where he wants them. The old hymn "A Mighty Fortress Is Our God" gives the devil due credit when it says, "On earth is not his equal." Not you, and not me.

Sin lives in you and the devil plays on your sinful nature. The apostle Paul describes this struggle: "I find this law at work: When I want to do good, evil is present with me. I certainly delight in God's law according to my inner self, but I see a different law at work in my members, waging war against the law of my mind and taking me captive to the law of sin, which is present in my members. What a miserable wretch I am! Who will rescue me from this body of death?" (Romans 7:21-24).

If that were the end of the story, you would have no hope. No hope of being free from fear and anxiety. Worse, no hope of a life without sin. No hope of heaven. You would have to stop reading right now. But you do have hope. The same old hymn, "A Mighty Fortress Is Our God," helps us to see clearly that hope: "But for us fights the valiant one." It's the one who has already won the battle. Paul had asked "Who will rescue me?" Paul answers his own question, "I thank God through Jesus Christ our Lord!" (Romans 7:25). He's your hope.

TWO

The Foundation

*"Always be prepared to give an answer
to everyone who asks you to give a reason
for the hope that is in you."*
1 Peter 3:15

What is the hope we have? Heaven. What is the reason for the hope we have? Jesus Christ.

In *Hope and Help for Your Nerves*, Weekes talks about your *staff*. Your staff is the thing you can rely on if you forget everything else when coping with anxiety. And what is this staff she referred to? Your staff is the fact that none of this matters. It doesn't matter if you cope with anxiety correctly. It doesn't matter if you ever conquer anxiety. She was correct again. It doesn't matter. But again, she didn't have the full story. Why doesn't it matter? Wise King Solomon has told us. "'Nothing but vapor,' Ecclesiastes said. 'Totally vapor. Everything is just vapor that vanishes'" (Ecclesiastes 1:2).

At the time of Adam and Eve's first sin, God had something to say to someone other than our first parents. He spoke to the serpent, that is, the devil. After cursing the serpent, God followed up with his gospel promise: "I will put hostility between you and the woman, and between your seed and her seed. He will crush your head, and you will crush his heel" (Genesis 3:15).

God promised a devil-crushing Savior who would save us from sin, death, and hell—and Jesus did just that. This is our foundation upon which everything is built. John's gospel encapsulates this gospel promise in one verse: "For God so loved the world that he gave his only-begotten Son, that whoever believes in him shall not perish, but have eternal life" (John 3:16). When it comes to our salvation, nothing more needs to be or can be done. Jesus did it all and proclaimed it with certainty on the cross when he said, "It is finished!" (John 19:30). This is why nothing else in this life really matters. This is why you don't have to be afraid. "There is no fear in love, but complete love drives out fear, because fear has to do with punishment" (1 John 4:18). There will be no punishment for those who believe in Jesus as their Savior. Why? Because God punished Jesus instead of us.

God, being a just God, demands payment for sins. We've all sinned; therefore we all have sins that must be paid for. That's a terrifying thought when you read the Bible's description of hell (okay, now you can panic). But wait! Because of God's grace and mercy, he sent his own Son, Jesus Christ, to pay for our sins so we don't have to make that impossible payment.

What sense does this make to our earthly minds? What kind of love is this? It's unfathomable. "At the appointed time, while we were still helpless, Christ died for the ungodly. It is rare indeed that someone will die for a righteous person. Perhaps someone might actually go so far as to die for a person who has been good to him. But God shows his own love for us in this: While we were still sinners, Christ died for us" (Romans 5:6-8).

Jesus, the perfect one, "has been tempted in every way, just as we are, yet was without sin" (Hebrews 4:15). But God placed on the perfect one all our sins, trespasses, and iniquities. The perfect suffers for the imperfect. Jesus, our substitute, lives the perfect life we never have, then suffers the punishment meant for us. He's the fulfillment of everything. That's grace. That's mercy.

I like this distinction between grace and mercy: Grace is getting what you don't deserve (eternal life); mercy is not getting what you deserve (punishment for our sins). It can all be summed up in God's incomprehensible love for us in Jesus Christ.

So all of our sins, including anxiety, have been paid in full. The victory is won! By faith in this promise, eternal life is ours. A perfect life, a life without anxiety, a life without sin—we won't find it this world. But it *is* ours in the world to come. And what can take you away from this eternal life? Your earthly problems? Your anxiety? Your failures? Paul writes, "If God is for us, who can be against us? Indeed, he who did not spare his own Son, but gave him up for us all—how will he not also graciously give us all things along with him?" (Romans 8:31,32). With God being for us and giving us his best in his Son, Jesus, what can take us away from him and what he's done? Paul continues: "What will separate us from the love of Christ? Will trouble or distress or persecution or famine or nakedness or danger or sword? Just as it is written: For your sake we are being put to death all day long. We are considered as sheep to be slaughtered. No, in all these things we are more than conquerors through him who loved us. For I am convinced that neither death nor life, neither angels nor rulers, neither things present nor things to come, nor powerful forces, neither height nor depth, nor anything else in creation, will be able to separate us from the love of God in Christ Jesus our Lord" (Romans 8:35-39).

Notice the progression in Paul's argument. He argues from the lesser to the greater (from trouble to sword), from the small problems to the big problems—nothing can separate us from God's love for us in Jesus. And to put those sufferings into perspective, Paul also writes, "I conclude that our sufferings at the present time are not worth comparing with the glory that is going to be revealed to us" (Romans 8:18). Next time you feel anxious, remember these words from your loving God (Romans 5:12,15).

Our foundation, the thing we always go back to, is this: We are saved through Jesus Christ. We can do nothing to save ourselves, and nothing in this life can separate us from the love of God found in Christ Jesus. When we falter in this life, we remember that Jesus has already won the only war that matters. He's the victor over sin, death, and the devil. He's assured us eternal life in heaven! Our life on earth is only a brief and temporary home. Our true home awaits us. Some have said that you need to lose your fear of death to conquer panic. There definitely is truth to that statement, but not for the reasons they think. Here's the truth: The Christian's earthly death leads to eternal life. We don't need to fear death. Jesus provides our foundation; he's the hope we have.

THREE

God's Discipline

"My son, do not regard the Lord's discipline lightly,
and do not become weary of his correction.
For the Lord disciplines the one whom he loves,
and he corrects every son he accepts."
Hebrews 12:5,6

The reason we suffer with anxiety is because of sin. You've probably asked the question "Why?" Why does God allow anxiety to happen to us? If God loves us so much that he gave his only Son for us, why would he allow anxiety and suffering to come into our lives? It's due to God's abounding love for us.

If you have children, or if you can remember when you were a child, you know that discipline is essential in a child's upbringing. We discipline our kids because we love them. Discipline has a way of shaping them. It leads them away from wrongdoing in the long run. Do our children understand this? Did *we* understand when our parents said no to us? The book of Proverbs speaks to parental discipline several times and is pretty direct when it says, "A person who withholds his rod hates his son, but one who loves him administers discipline promptly" (Proverbs 13:24). "Discipline your son while there is hope. Do not make yourself responsible for his death" (Proverbs 19:18). "Do not withhold discipline from a child, for if you strike him with a rod, he will not die. Strike him yourself with a rod, and you will rescue his soul from death" (Proverbs 23:13,14). "Discipline your son, and he will give you rest. He will give delight to your soul" (Proverbs 29:17).

Our heavenly Father, the perfect parent, disciplines us for our good to draw us closer to himself. He allows anxiety to come into our lives because he loves us. He's treating us as his children whom he loves. The Bible says, "Do not reject the LORD's discipline, my son, and do not despise his warning, because the LORD warns the one he loves as a father warns a son with whom he is pleased" (Proverbs 3:11,12). My encouragement to you is to view hardship as discipline. In this light, your struggle with anxiety is a positive experience. The letter to the Hebrew believers addresses the topic of discipline to believers who were experiencing difficulties in their Christian lives, "Endure suffering as discipline. God is dealing with you as sons. Is there a son whose father does not discipline him? If you are not disciplined (and all of us have received it), then you are illegitimate children and not sons. In addition, we have earthly fathers who disciplined us, and we respected them. Should we not submit even more to the Father of the spirits and live? They disciplined us for a little while, according to what seemed best to them, but God disciplines us for our good, so that we may have a share in his holiness" (Hebrews 12:7-10).

What's your typical view of discipline? Love it? Embrace it? Relish it? If you are like me, our natural instinct is to hate it and avoid it at all cost. But that's our sinful nature speaking to us. How about this instead:

View anxiety as discipline to be a positive experience in your life—probably the most positive experience you will ever have. God uses anxiety for your good. He's disciplining you. Is it pleasant? Not at the time. In fact, the Hebrew Christians also heard this: "No discipline seems pleasant when it is happening, but painful, yet later it yields a peaceful harvest of righteousness for those who have been trained by it" (Hebrews 12:11).

When our parents disciplined us, there was pain. It may have been physical or emotional, but it was used to alter our behavior. Yet that pain we experienced during discipline has a way of subsiding, even to the point where it is difficult to remember. We may not remember the pain, but we're different. That's the *later* time mentioned in the Hebrews passage above. Discipline changes us.

God wants changes when it comes to our faith. He doesn't want us to remain infants in the faith. God wants growth, he wants strong faith, and he's doing something to make that happen. He's working for our good. He wants us to trust in him, not ourselves. The apostle Peter knew Christians in Asia Minor were experiencing difficulties and needed reminders about God's discipline, just like we do. He wrote, "Because of this you rejoice very much, even though now for a little while, if necessary, you have been grieved by various kinds of trials so that the proven character of your faith—which is more valuable than gold, which passes away even though it is tested by fire—may be found to result in praise, glory, and honor when Jesus Christ is revealed" (1 Peter 1:6,7).

God knows what's best for us. Many times, this can be contrary to what *we* think is best for us. There's that sinful nature again. Paul writes, "We know that all things work together for the good of those who love God, for those who are called according to his purpose" (Romans 8:28). *All* things. How hard that is for us to remember! When we don't remember that *all* things work for our good, aren't we forgetting what Jesus told us when he said, "Are not two sparrows sold for a small coin? Yet not one of them will fall to the ground without the knowledge and consent of your Father. And even the hairs of your head are all numbered. So do not be afraid. You are worth more than many sparrows" (Matthew 10:29-31). Numbered hairs, perfect knowledge about us, and of great worth to God—how can we forget this?

We know God loves us. He gave up his Son to rescue us . . . he must love us! Paul writes, "He who did not spare his own Son, but gave him up for us all—how will he not also graciously give us all things along with him?" (Romans 8:32). And think how great your faithful heavenly Father's love is for you, if even flawed human fathers know how to take care of their children. Jesus says, "Who among you, if his son asks him for bread, would give him a stone? Or who, if his son asks for a fish, would give him a snake? Then if you know how to give good gifts to your children, even though you are evil, how much more will your Father in heaven give good gifts to those who ask him!" (Matthew 7:9-11).

At some point, take the time to read the book of Job. It's the story of a man who had everything, lost everything (from a worldly perspective), and then ended up with much more than he started with. He ended up with a stronger faith. In the midst of his suffering he confidently states, "As for me, I know that my Redeemer lives, and that at the end of time he will stand over the dust. Then, even after my skin has been destroyed, nevertheless, in my own flesh I will see God" (Job 19:25,26). Be assured that is God's promise for all of us, his disciplined children. In Job's case, God blessed him greatly in this life as well, after he experienced significant hardship. Job is a story of God the Father disciplining one of his sons with struggles. God uses Job's struggles for his good, drawing Job ever closer to him and leading Job to see God is in control. Job himself said, "How blessed is the man whom God corrects! Do not reject the discipline of the Almighty! For though he may inflict wounds, he also bandages them. Though he may strike, his hands also heal" (Job 5:17,18). Discipline, difficulty, anxiety . . . how blessed we are when God corrects!

Viewing anxiety in a positive light is not easy. The devil will try to convince you otherwise. Your way out of anxiety is always the same: Trust that your heavenly Father always disciplines you for your own good. Rejoice in it!

The apostle Paul learned to rejoice in discipline. Paul, like you and me, had a problem. He called it a thorn in his flesh. I have always wondered what Paul's thorn was. God never told us the answer. Could he have struggled with anxiety? It doesn't really matter. God used this thorn to discipline Paul. Paul goes into detail about experiencing this discipline from God:

> To keep me from becoming arrogant due to the extraordinary nature of these revelations, I was given a thorn in my flesh, a messenger of Satan, to torment me, so that I would not become arrogant. Three times I pleaded with the Lord about this, that he would take it away from me. And he said to me, "My grace is sufficient for you, because my power is made perfect in weakness." Therefore I will be glad to boast all the more in my weaknesses, so that the power of Christ may shelter me. That is why I delight in weaknesses, in insults, in hardships, in persecutions, in difficulties, for the sake of Christ. For whenever I am weak, then am I strong. (2 Corinthians 12:7-10)

There's so much we could say about these verses. I refer to them often, and they give me great comfort. Notice how Paul knows that God uses this thorn to help him trust God and not himself. This is the cornerstone of God's discipline. God uses discipline and hardship to draw us closer to himself and strengthen our faith. We learn to rely on God, not ourselves. And look how this affected Paul to look away from himself and to rely on his Lord—Paul goes so far to even boast about his own weaknesses. Why? Because Christ's power shelters him. When Paul knows he's weak and acknowledges that he depends totally on God, Christ's power shines and shelters him. It's then that his thorn no longer has a hold on him. His weakness becomes his strength. He learns to trust in the power of God, not in himself.

God disciplines us through our hardships. Our God of love does not set out to destroy us, but to strengthen our faith. The psalmist writes, "It was good for me that I was afflicted, so that I might learn your statutes" (Psalm 119:71). And where are these statutes found? They are found only in God's Word . . . what God uses to strengthen us.

FOUR

God's Promises

*"No temptation has overtaken you except what is
common to mankind. And God is faithful; he will not
let you be tempted beyond what you can bear.
But when you are tempted, he will also provide
a way out so that you can endure it."*
1 Corinthians 10:13

The last chapter talked about God's discipline.
Because God loves you, you can view anxiety in
a positive light of God disciplining you. God disciplines you to strengthen your faith in him, to draw
you to himself, to help you realize your own sinful-
ness and helplessness so that you trust in him, and
to ultimately save you and give you eternal life in
heaven. God's discipline is not pleasant at the time.

So how do you deal with anxiety, and even panic, when those unpleasant moments come? The answer is, You don't have to.

Claire Weekes talked about dealing with anxiety through Facing, Accepting, Floating, and Letting Time Pass. As we said in chapter 2, we can accept anxiety because we know nothing in this world really matters. We don't have to be afraid of it. Nothing can separate us from the love of God in Christ Jesus. We are saved from our sins because of Jesus Christ, and eternal life in heaven awaits us. Facing anxiety is not an easy thing to do. Discipline is not pleasant. Our natural instinct is to run away from it—to avoid it. Weekes argued that if you could see anxiety as a mere physical reaction, something totally harmless, you could lose your fear of it. Instead of fleeing from anxiety, instead of trying to change it, face it and accept it. See it for what it is, a harmless physical reaction.

As I said in the preface of this book, any help for my anxiety had to be consistent with God's Word. And in 1 Corinthians, I found it. "No temptation has overtaken you except what is common to mankind. And God is faithful; he will not let you be tempted beyond what you can bear. But when you are tempted, he will also provide a way out so that you can endure it" (1 Corinthians 10:13 NIV). This passage, maybe more than any other, gave me tremendous comfort in understanding anxiety and dealing with it. It helped me realize that Weekes' teachings were correct. I could face those moments of panic because they would never be more than I could bear. But I had something way more than the teaching of Claire Weekes—I had the promise of God. And now, I had the power of God.

In 1 Corinthians 10:13, God told me that *he* would not give me more than I could bear. He promises this to all of us. I came to realize that anxiety was something I could deal with. I could face it and accept it. Why? Because *I* didn't have to deal with it. God promises that *he* would deal with it for me. "God is faithful." "*He* will not let you be tempted beyond what you can bear." "*He* will also provide a way out." God was showing me that *he* is in control. I need to trust in *him*. *He* is my way out!

If you study the 1 Corinthians passage further, you will find more comfort in the last few words. When we think of finding a way out of a situation, we often think of somehow fleeing from it. We think we need to flee to a place of safety, but fleeing is exactly what we should *not* do when dealing with anxiety. What does God promise us? That he will help us flee from it? No! He promises "a way out so that *you can endure it.*" He promises safety in the situation. He gives us the ability to face anxiety and remain in the situation. And now I see the consistency with what Weekes was saying. God's promises tie directly into the Facing and Accepting, and even Floating.

When those moments of pain come, that is when "the power of Christ may shelter me" (2 Corinthians 12:9). This is from the "thorn" passage referred to in the previous chapter, Paul's realization that he can rejoice in his weaknesses. Why? Because that is when Paul sees God's power working in his life. God's promises, contained in his Word, are true. This is how our faith in God is strengthened! *He* will help me stay in the situation—to stand and face it, as well as accept it.

It won't be more than I can bear! *He* promises this in the 1 Corinthians passage. And now Paul goes on to say, "For whenever I am weak, then am I strong" (2 Corinthians 12:10).

The apostle Paul said, "I am not saying this because I lack anything; in fact, I have learned to be content in any circumstances in which I find myself. I know what it is to live in humble circumstances, and I know what it is to have more than enough. I have learned the secret of being content in any and every situation, while being full or hungry, while having plenty or not enough. I can do all things through Christ, who strengthens me" (Philippians 4:11-13). Paul could stay in any situation. Why? Because *God* gave him the strength to do so. Paul knew it would never be more than he could bear. He was convinced that Christ would strengthen him. God promises this to all of us. The Lord assures us, "Do not fear, for I am with you. Do not be overwhelmed, for I am your God. I will strengthen you. Yes, I will help you. I will uphold you with my righteous right hand" (Isaiah 41:10).

You may say that the 1 Corinthians passage only refers to temptation. We don't often think of fear and temptation as being closely related. But when Jesus was tempted by the devil, he was being tempted to sin—to disown God (see Luke 4). When anxiety comes upon us, we are being tempted to sin—to disown God and turn away from him. God promises us that when those moments come along, *he* will be with us. Trust his Word and turn to him! "Submit yourselves to God. Resist the Devil, and he will flee from you. Come near to God, and he will come near to you" (James 4:7,8).

God rescues us from sin! His ultimate rescue came when he rescued us from the sentence of hell, when he sent his Son to die for us and rise again. That's our foundation. Now we can build on that foundation. God also rescues us in our earthly struggles with sin. "Because he clings to me, I will rescue him. I will protect him, because he acknowledges my name. He will call on me, and I will answer him. I will be with him in distress. I will deliver him and I will honor him" (Psalm 91:14,15). Notice the pronoun God uses: I, I, I, I! God will do it for us.

When those moments of anxiety come, do we need to look to ourselves to remember all this? No! The Spirit, working through the Word, reminds us of God's promise. And he takes our hearts to a place of peace. On the night before he died, Jesus promised, "Peace I leave with you. My peace I give to you. Not as the world gives do I give to you. Do not let your heart be troubled, and do not let it be afraid" (John 14:27). God gives us the wisdom and understanding we need in every situation.

Reflect back on a time of high anxiety in your life. Did you stay afraid? God rescued you! He's faithful to his promises. The Bible asks, "Now what if some did not believe? Their unbelief will not nullify God's faithfulness, will it? Absolutely not!" (Romans 3:3,4). The Bible also says, "If we are faithless, he remains faithful, because he cannot deny himself" (2 Timothy 2:13). God's promises can be relied on, always.

Remember the story of Peter walking on the water toward Jesus. What happened during the water-walking episode? "When he saw the strong wind, he was afraid. As he began to sink, he cried out, 'Lord, save me!' Immediately Jesus stretched out his hand, took hold of him, and said to him, 'You of little faith, why did you doubt?'" (Matthew 14:30,31). Why doubt? God is faithful. His Word is true. Our peace comes from God (James 1:17)!

Our way out of anxiety is found in the promises of God's Word. The Bible says, "I will not break off my mercy from him. I will not let my truth become false. I will not violate my covenant. I will not alter what comes out of my lips" (Psalm 89:33,34). God's mercy stands through every difficulty; his promises never break.

FIVE

Perseverance

"Not only so, but we also rejoice in our sufferings,
because we know that suffering produces perseverance;
perseverance, character; and character, hope.
And hope does not put us to shame, because God's
love has been poured into our hearts through
the Holy Spirit, who has been given to us."

Romans 5:3-5 NIV

The passage above starts with suffering and ends with hope. The Bible says, "Always be prepared to give an answer to everyone who asks you to give a reason for the hope that is in you" (1 Peter 3:15). What is the hope we have? Heaven. What is the reason for the hope we have? Jesus Christ. It's the foundation, again. "Faith is being sure about what we hope for, being convinced about things we do not see" (Hebrews 11:1).

The passage above from Romans says to "rejoice in our sufferings." Why? Look what it leads to: not destruction, but hope! God hasn't allowed suffering to come into your life to destroy you. He uses it to draw you to himself. He uses it to strengthen your faith. Remember, "We know that all things work together for the good of those who love God, for those who are called according to his purpose" (Romans 8:28). All things! Yes, that means even sufferings.

Rejoicing in the face of suffering isn't easy. It's so contrary to our sinful way of thinking. It's hard for us to see the good in the bad. And then to rejoice when it's bad? That almost seems sadistic. Why would we want to rejoice and be happy about suffering? James helps to ground us in the blessings of God when we suffer. He wrote, "Consider it pure joy, my brothers and sisters, whenever you face trials of many kinds, because you know that the testing of your faith produces perseverance. Let perseverance finish its work so that you may be mature and complete, not lacking anything" (James 1:2-4 NIV). And to further spot-light blessings in trials, he goes on to write, "Blessed is the one who perseveres under trial because, having stood the test, that person will receive the crown of life that the Lord has promised to those who love him" (James 1:12 NIV).

You've seen the word *perseverance* in several of the passages above. It's a word whose true biblical meaning is very much misunderstood. In the sinful society around us, when we refer to people who persevere, we often think of individuals who push through the hard times, who buck up under the pressure, and who dig deep down inside themselves for strength. That's not biblical perseverance; that view of perseverance isn't what God is telling us. It's just the opposite. When the Bible speaks about perseverance, it's about trusting in God—persevering in the faith. Not trusting in ourselves. Using an image of a tree under duress to teach about trust in the Lord, Jeremiah writes, "Blessed is anyone who trusts in the Lord, whose confidence is in him. He will be like a tree planted by water. It sends out its roots to the stream. It does not fear the heat when it comes. Its leaves will remain green. It is not concerned about a time of drought. It does not stop producing fruit" (Jeremiah 17:7,8). The psalmist confidently confesses his trust in God in the face of fear: "On the day when I am afraid, I will trust in you. In God I praise his word. In God I trust. I will not fear: What can flesh do to me?" (Psalm 56:3,4). Perseverance means staying connected with the Savior through faith.

Dealing with anxiety is always a positive thing! Claire Weekes said it gives you the opportunity to practice. For the Christian, what will you get to practice? You get to practice trusting in God, trusting his Word. *Persevering* in the faith is your opportunity to see God's power—to see God strengthen your faith. In turn, you gain wisdom and understanding. It's what God desires for us. The poetic book of Proverbs says, "Acquire wisdom. Acquire understanding. Do not forget, and do not turn away from the words of my mouth. Do not abandon it, and it will watch over you. Love it and it will guard you" (Proverbs 4:5,6).

Joy . . . rejoice . . . delight . . . God connects these words to hardships and suffering. Why? Through hardships and sufferings, the Holy Spirit teaches you to trust in God. Through the Holy Spirit, you see that God's Word is true. Through that Word, he strengthens us. We have reasons to rejoice when the Spirit deepens our connection to our Savior (1 Peter 1:6,7).

Anxiety is always a positive thing! Remember this when you have moments of anxiety after long periods without anxiety. God's drawing you to himself. He's disciplining you. He's strengthening your faith. He's reminding you that *he* is in control. He's reminding you to trust in *him*. And, oh, do we need the reminder (John 14:26)! Our sinful nature would love to forget all these blessings. So we need to be reminded of this over and over again, until our faith is "mature and complete, not lacking anything" (James 1:4). Faith complete? Faith not lacking anything? You know when that time is, don't you? That's not until we reach heaven. Paul writes, "There is one thing I do [know]: Forgetting the things that are behind and straining toward the things that are ahead, I press on toward the goal, for the prize of the upward call of God in Christ Jesus" (Philippians 3:13,14). This is perseverance!

Many passages in the Bible speak to perseverance. "Brothers and sisters, as an example of patience in the face of suffering, take the prophets who spoke in the name of the Lord. As you know, we count as blessed those who have *persevered*. You have heard of Job's *perseverance* and have seen what the Lord finally brought about. The Lord is full of compassion and mercy" (James 5:10,11 NIV, emphasis added). "You need to *persevere* so that when you have done the will of God, you will receive what he has promised" (Hebrews 10:36 NIV, emphasis added). "By faith he left Egypt, not fearing the king's anger; he *persevered* because he saw him who is invisible" (Hebrews 11:27 NIV, emphasis added). "You have *persevered* and have endured hardships for my name, and have not grown weary" (Revelation 2:3 NIV, emphasis added). "The seed on good soil stands for those with a noble and good heart, who hear the word, retain it, and by *persevering* produce a crop" (Luke 8:15 NIV, emphasis added).

Perseverance is trusting in God. *Perseverance* is relying on God's promises, contained in his Word—always (Hebrews 5:14). God's Word is your weapon in your moments of pain. It's all you need. This is how you *persevere*. And remember, it is not you. It is the Holy Spirit working in you, working your heart to trust in him.

Listen how God outfits and arms us to persevere: Finally, be strong in the Lord and in his mighty power. Put on the full armor of God, so that you can stand against the schemes of the Devil. For our struggle is not against flesh and blood, but against the rulers, against the authorities, against the world rulers of this darkness, against the spiritual forces of evil in the heavenly places. For this reason, take up the full armor of God, so that you will be able to take a stand on the evil day and, after you have done everything, to stand. Stand, then, with the belt of truth buckled around your waist, with the breastplate of righteousness fastened in place, and with the readiness that comes from the gospel of peace tied to your feet like sandals. At all times hold up the shield of faith, with which you will be able to extinguish all the flaming arrows of the Evil One. Also take the helmet of salvation and the sword of the Spirit, which is the word of God. (Ephesians 6:10-17)

Do you recognize that word *stand* in the passage above? Remember God's promise that we discussed in chapter 4? "But when you are tempted, he will also provide a way out so that you can endure it" (1 Corinthians 10:13 NIV).

Our struggle is not against anxiety. Whether we ever overcome anxiety or not, it doesn't matter. This is our foundation again. Our struggle is against the evil one, who tries to take us away from God and tries to place doubts in our minds and remove our faith. "You belong to your father, the Devil, and you want to do your father's desires. He was a murderer from the beginning and did not remain standing in the truth, because there is no truth in him. Whenever he lies, he speaks from what is his, because he is a liar and the father of lying" (John 8:44). When the evil one comes, we can stand and not run away. Why? Because the evil one is powerless in the face of God. We have the power of God, through faith in his Word, which "extinguish[es] all the flaming arrows of the Evil One" (Ephesians 6:16; James 4:7,8). When faced against an enemy determined to destroy it, Israel was told, "The LORD will fight for you. You must wait quietly" (Exodus 14:14).

So much of anxiety is related to our ability to attach meaning to meaningless things. That is, to focus on lies instead of truth. The devil endlessly tries to confuse us by planting lies in our minds. The "belt of truth" is found in God's Word. God's Word is truth! The Bible says, "Sanctify them by the truth. Your word is truth" (John 17:17). When anxiety comes, use the "sword of the Spirit, which is the word of God." This is how you persevere. God's "truth will set you free" (John 8:32).

Jesus showed us the power of the Word at work. Every time the devil attacked with a temptation, Jesus said, "It is written." He turned to the truth and power found only in God's Word. The devil's flaming arrows were extinguished, and the devil eventually left him.

"Finally, brothers, whatever is true, whatever is honorable, whatever is right, whatever is pure, whatever is lovely, whatever is commendable, if anything is excellent, and if anything is praiseworthy, think about these things. The things that you learned, received, heard, and saw in me: Keep doing these things. And the God of peace will be with you" (Philippians 4:8,9). "Keep doing these things." That's perseverance. That's using what works with anxiety, the Word of Truth.

SIX

God Is in Control

"Every good act of giving and every perfect gift is from above, coming down from the Father of the lights, who does not change or shift like a shadow."

James 1:17

It is so hard to take the focus off us. In moments of pain, we often think of what we have to do to fight anxiety. Books contain all sorts of tricks to do when anxiety comes along. If the authors only knew . . . the answer is nothing.

Look around and you will see people with great confidence in themselves. Many of them have never dealt with the pain we deal with. Do I want to be like them and have great confidence? Yes! But the difference is where I want my confidence to come from. "Blessed is anyone who trusts in the LORD, whose confidence is in him" (Jeremiah 17:7). My confidence is in the One who never changes, the One who is always strong. My confidence is in my God—trusting the truths of his Word. How painful and always disappointing it is for those who trust in themselves! In moments of great pain, what can we do to help ourselves? Who can bear this burden? "Trust in the LORD with all your heart, and do not rely on your own understanding. In all your ways acknowledge him, and he will make your paths straight" (Proverbs 3:5,6).

In dark times, we may feel forsaken and forgotten by God, but the only one on this side of heaven who has ever been totally forsaken by God is Jesus Christ on the cross. "About the ninth hour Jesus cried out with a loud voice, saying, '*Eli, Eli, lama sabachthani?*' which means 'My God, my God, why have you forsaken me?'" (Matthew 27:46). God the Father laid the sins of the whole world on his Son Jesus and turned his back on him. No rescue from his Father.

And there you have true hell: the total absence of God's love.

In this life, God has promised that will never happen to us. "Do not be afraid, for I am with you" (Genesis 26:24). "I will never leave you, and I will never forsake you" (Hebrews 13:5). God is always with us! God rescues us! He holds out his hand and faithfully pulls us back to himself when we fall! The Lord states with certainty that he will do this. Notice how many times he leaves no doubt when he says "I will" in Psalm 91: "Because he clings to me, I will rescue him. I will protect him, because he acknowledges my name. He will call on me, and I will answer him. I will be with him in distress. I will deliver him and I will honor him. With long life I will satisfy him, and I will let him see my salvation" (Psalm 91:14-16).

So why do we doubt? Why are we so afraid? Let's get into two fishing boats to watch and listen to Jesus on the Sea of Galilee. During a wavy boat ride, Peter wanted to walk out onto the water to be with Jesus. With the urging of Jesus, Peter steps out onto the watery surface and walks. But then Peter's eyes take in the wind, whipping water and waves. His eyes of faith looked away from Jesus. "As he began to sink, he cried out, 'Lord, save me!'" (Matthew 14:30). Then what happens? Does Jesus allow him to drown? No! "Immediately Jesus stretched out his hand, took hold of him, and said to him, 'You of little faith, *why did you doubt?*'" (Matthew 14:31, emphasis added). Why did you doubt Peter?

In another water excursion, waves splash, crash, and dump buckets of water into a boat filled with panic-stricken disciples and a peaceful-sleeping Jesus. Afraid they will soon be at the bottom of the Sea of Galilee, the disciples wake Jesus. "'Teacher, don't you care that we are about to drown?' Then he got up, rebuked the wind, and said to the sea, 'Peace! Be still!' The wind stopped, and there was a great calm. He said to them, 'Why are you so afraid? Do you still lack faith?'" (Mark 4:38-40). Why are you so afraid, disciples? Where's your faith?

Why do we doubt? Why are we so afraid? Why do we lack faith? Storms of trouble will come into our lives; we will be afraid; we will doubt. But Jesus' questions tell us, "Don't you understand? I am in control. I will never leave you and will rescue you from all your troubles. Trust in me!" Jesus promises us peace through him. "I have told you these things, so that you may have peace in me. In this world you are going to have trouble. But be courageous! I have overcome the world" (John 16:33).

Our God overcomes the world. God's leaders and people in the Old Testament didn't just face storms of rain but threats to their lives and future existence as God brought them into the Promised Land. When they faced seemingly insurmountable odds and enemies, the Lord promised he was in control and would never forsake them. Read these words with a heart that hears the same words of promise when odds, enemies, and anxiety seem to be stacked up against you. "Be strong and courageous. Do not be afraid and do not be terrified before them, because the LORD your God is going with you. He will not abandon you and he will not forsake you" (Deuteronomy 31:6). "The LORD himself will go ahead of you. He will be with you. He will not abandon you, and he will not forsake you. Do not be afraid and do not be over-whelmed" (Deuteronomy 31:8). "No one will be able to stand against you all the days of your life. Just as I was with Moses, I will be with you. I will not abandon you, and I will not forsake you" (Joshua 1:5). God is in control.

We don't need to recognize God's control only in the difficult times. He's there in the good times, the happy moments, and the times we are at peace. "Every good act of giving and every perfect gift is from above, coming down from the Father of the lights, who does not change or shift like a shadow" (James 1:17). He has always been there for us. Sometimes we didn't know or remember these were all from him too.

God's Spirit works with God's promises to bring us along in our faith. Spirit-worked faith grows and grips onto God's controlling hand that stills all storms and sets the sun in the sky to shine on every new day. Spirit-worked faith grasps that same hand of God that controls all personal storms and peace-filled moments in life. Spirit-worked faith won't ever want to let go of these words from Paul: "The Lord is near. Do not worry about anything, but in everything, by prayer and petition, with thanksgiving, let your requests be made known to God. And the peace of God, which surpasses all understanding, will guard your hearts and your minds in Christ Jesus" (Philippians 4:5-7).

SEVEN

God's Love

"For God so loved the world that he gave his only-begotten Son, that whoever believes in him shall not perish, but have eternal life."

John 3:16

A man sacrifices his life for the woman he loves. A mother gives every ounce of strength to protect her child. The bond of siblings stands up to those who seek to harm one. Deep-seated human love for another soul astounds us when we see it in action. How about God's love for us? Unfathomable. Incomprehensible. Deeper than we could ever begin to grasp. Paul prays that the Ephesian Christians take into their hearts and minds the expansiveness of God's love: "Being rooted and grounded in love, I pray that you would be able to comprehend, along with all the saints, how wide and long and high and deep his love is, and that you would be able to know the love of Christ that surpasses knowledge, so that you may be filled to all the fullness of God" (Ephesians 3:17-19). Paul wants the Ephesian Christians and us not to think of God's love as a shallow kiddie pool but to picture it like a vast ocean trench, impossible to ever fully explore. Paul wants them and us to know that Christ's love goes beyond what our brains could ever process or take in.

But God's love goes far beyond this earth. If your faith in God only gains you freedom from fear in this life, what have you gained? His love impacts our eternity. Jesus took on flesh to become one of us. He stepped up to substitute himself for sinners. He saved souls through his perfection and through an undeserved hellish punishment. He states his victory for us when he marched out alive from his stone tomb. He wins us life eternal. That's love. That's out-of-this-world love. That's our foundation.

Because of God's great love for us, he cares for us in what could be classified as our minute and meaningless earthly experiences. He knows what we need and when we need it. He's told us so. "So do not worry, saying, 'What will we eat?' or 'What will we drink?' or 'What will we wear?' For the unbelievers chase after all these things. Certainly your heavenly Father knows that you need all these things. But seek first the kingdom of God and his righteousness, and all these things will be given to you as well" (Matthew 6:31-33). God knows our every need! That's love.

What about our struggles, our temptations, and our times when anxiety threatens to overtake us? Does God see it? Does he understand what we're going through? Jesus, the God-man, can relate and understands. "We do not have a high priest who is unable to sympathize with our weaknesses, but one who has been tempted in every way, just as we are, yet was without sin. So let us approach the throne of grace with confidence, so that we may receive mercy and find grace to help in time of need" (Hebrews 4:15,16). Earlier in that same book, God says, "Because he suffered when he was tempted, he is able to help those who are being tempted" (Hebrews 2:18). He sympathizes with us and stands ready to help. That's love.

Remember what Jesus said about birds and us human beings. Birds don't farm or fill up barns, but they have all they need from the heavenly Father. The smallest of sparrows die, and God knows about that life. You are worth far more than birds. The hairs on your head are numbered, which means God sees every part of you down to the smallest detail. Nothing about you goes unnoticed. No need to worry (Matthew 6:26,27; 10:29-31). Now think about the times when you suffered. Remember how God rescued you and brought you through the suffering! The apostle Paul reflected on God's rescuing help when he wrote, "The kind of persecutions I endured—and the Lord rescued me from all of them" (2 Timothy 3:11).

With his knowledge that spans eternity, God knew you before you were formed in your mother's womb. The Lord pointed this out to the prophet Jeremiah (Jeremiah 1:5). And God didn't just know you; he chose you to be his own. We have certainty.

The God who never lies puts his reputation on the line and states emphatically what he all does. Check out how many times he uses the pronoun *I* in this passage filled with promises to us. "[You] whom I have snatched from the ends of the earth, whom I have called from its corners—I have said to you, 'You are my servant.' I have chosen you and not rejected you. Do not fear, for I am with you. Do not be overwhelmed, for I am your God. I will strengthen you. Yes, I will help you. I will uphold you with my righteous right hand" (Isaiah 41:9,10). He snatches us up, calls us, chooses us, strengthens us, helps us, and upholds us with his holy hand. God determined that he would do this for you all before you were born. That's comforting. That's love.

The Bible piles on promise after promise that you, dear Christian, can find great comfort: God chose you (predestined) before day 1 of this created world. Listen to these passages of promise: "Because those God foreknew, he also predestined to be conformed to the image of his Son, so that he would be the first-born among many brothers. And those he predestined, he also called. Those he called, he also justified. And those he justified, he also glorified. What then will we say about these things? If God is for us, who can be against us? Indeed, he who did not spare his own Son, but gave him up for us all—how will he not also graciously give us all things along with him?" (Romans 8:29-32). "He did this when he chose us in Christ before the foundation of the world, so that we would be holy and blameless in his sight. In love he predestined us to be adopted as his sons through Jesus Christ. He did this in accordance with the good purpose of his will, and for the praise of his glorious grace, which he has graciously given us in the one he loves" (Ephesians 1:4-6). And later in that same chapter God says, "In him we have also obtained an inheritance, because we were predestined according to the plan of him who works out everything in keeping with the purpose of his will. He did this so that his glory would be praised as a result of us, who were the first to hope in Christ" (Ephesians 1:11,12). God predestined us. He planned it. That's love!

We are God's chosen children; he knows what's best for us. Our suffering will not destroy us; it's meant for our good. He has a plan for our lives on this earth and, more important, in the life to come. God loves us!

EIGHT

Our Thoughts

"'For my thoughts are not your thoughts,
neither are your ways my ways,' declares the LORD.
'As the heavens are higher than the earth,
so are my ways higher than your ways and
my thoughts than your thoughts.'"

Isaiah 55:8,9 NIV

I know that the man breaking into my house at night is a bad guy. I can see him. The soldier knows that the person firing a gun at him is his enemy. He can see him. But what if you can't see the attacker? What if the attack comes from within? Our thoughts—how we struggle with them. We want peace so badly. The more we want it, the farther away it seems from us. If only we could always do what the Bible urges us to do. "Finally, brothers, whatever is true, whatever is honorable, whatever is right, whatever is pure, whatever is lovely, whatever is commendable, if anything is excellent, and if anything is praiseworthy, *think about these things*" (Philippians 4:8, emphasis added). If only our thoughts would not be the bad guy or enemy within, but that we could be at peace thinking godly thoughts.

Although the Bible encourages and directs us to think about the God-pleasing things, we don't always do that. The apostle Paul knew about the war within. He knew that within him there was a war waging "against the law of [his] mind and taking [him] captive to the law of sin, which is present in [his] members" (Romans 7:23). Here lies our true struggle in this world. Your sinful nature teams up with the dark spiritual forces of evil and it's a battle. "For our struggle is not against flesh and blood, but against the rulers, against the authorities, against the world rulers of this darkness, against the spiritual forces of evil in the heavenly places" (Ephesians 6:12).

Weekes wrote about the tense hold we keep on ourselves when it comes to struggling with our anxiety, an internal battle. She noted that we watch to make sure panic doesn't come. We make sure we are thinking the right thoughts. Weekes is talking about fretting. The Bible says, "Do not fret—it leads only to evil" (Psalm 37:8). Do you see what fretting really is? It's trusting in ourselves. It's making sure we have the answer to every evil thought that comes into our mind. What a burden! What a battle!

The Bible describes a fight inside every Christian, the struggle between the new person and the old person. It's the ongoing struggle with sin we'll have until the day we die. Yet Paul finds something all of us want so desperately in every situation, in every struggle, in every wrestling match with anxiety, in every suffering with our thoughts. "I am not saying this because I lack anything; in fact, I have learned to be content in any circumstances in which I find myself. I know what it is to live in humble circumstances, and I know what it is to have more than enough. I have learned the secret of being content in any and every situation, while being full or hungry, while having plenty or not enough. I can do all things through Christ, who strengthens me" (Philippians 4:11-13). Christ strengthens Paul. But how about you? Does God still promise strength to you? "Do not fear, for I am with you. Do not be overwhelmed, for I am your God. I will strengthen you. Yes, I will help you. I will uphold you with my righteous right hand" (Isaiah 41:10). He's made promises. He strengthens and he helps.

Paul knows God's promises and trusts him, and God provides peace. "You preserve perfect peace for the person whose resolve is steadfast, because he trusts in you" (Isaiah 26:3). True peace comes only from God. "Peace I leave with you. My peace I give to you. Not as the world gives do I give to you. Do not let your heart be troubled, and do not let it be afraid" (John 14:27). For true peace to settle across our thoughts, it's the Lord who will need to do that.

To be our help in the battle in our anxious minds, to be our strength that allows us to carry on, and to bring peace to our thoughts, we need to go to the one place where these can be found. Paul encouraged the Philippians to think about "whatever is *true*." To the Ephesians, Paul urged them to be outfitted with "the belt of *truth* buckled around your waist." Here's the place; this is where our thoughts should reside: on the truth. And what is true? "God is true" (John 3:33). "Sanctify them by the truth. Your word is truth" (John 17:17). We find truth only in God and his Word. This is where all truth is found! In the truth of the Word, God brings us aid, endurance, and peace of mind.

And with those comes victory. Remember what Jesus did when the devil worked on Jesus' mind and heart to get him to fall? Every time the devil tempted him, Jesus said, "It is written" (see Matthew 4). Jesus used God's Word to counter the devil's lies. Jesus trusted in his heavenly Father; he trusted God's power through the use of the Word. Finally, when Jesus had taken every best shot the devil could dish out, after wielding the sword of the Spirit and the Word of God, the devil left him. Victory came to an embattled mind and heart through the Word.

God's Word is our weapon. The Holy Spirit strengthens faith through use of the Word. He builds our trust. Trust his power. Constant use of God's Word is the key! The Word helps us to see how sinful and powerless we are, but it also brings out how much God loves us. The Word brings the eyes of our faith to see battles, struggles, and hurts as a good thing. God disciplines us to strengthen us. He helps us to learn to trust him, not ourselves. In good times, it's easy to slip in our faith. It's in our moments of struggle when God displays his power, so we look to him.

Earlier, we heard Weekes advise us to accept anxiety when it comes. Accept the struggles and scary thoughts while you remember these promises, "No temptation has overtaken you except what is common to mankind. And God is faithful; he will not let you be tempted beyond what you can bear. But when you are tempted, he will also provide a way out so that you can endure it" (1 Corinthians 10:13). And remember this, "We know that all things work together for the good of those who love God, for those who are called according to his purpose" (Romans 8:28).

God gives us what we need at every moment. He may allow us to have fear, anxiety, or a restless mind. He may allow us to have confidence, calmness, and peace. Our Christian faith sees them all and says these are all good! These are perfect gifts from God. And "every perfect gift is from above, coming down from the Father of the lights, who does not change or shift like a shadow" (James 1:17). Wise King Solomon said, "On a good day, enjoy the good, but on a bad day, consider carefully. God has made the one as well as the other, so no man can find out about anything that will come later" (Ecclesiastes 7:14). God is in control and he loves us. When it comes to our thoughts, our loving Savior knows what is best for us. "Be still, and know that I am God" (Psalm 46:10). Be at ease in your mind because of his promise. Be at rest in your thoughts because Jesus promises you, "Come to me all you who are weary and burdened, and I will give you rest" (Matthew 11:28).

NINE

Living Your Life

"When I was a child, I spoke like a child, I thought like
a child, I reasoned like a child. When I became a man,
I put away childish things."

1 Corinthians 13:11

Children of God, sons and daughters of the King, coheirs with Christ—that's who we are. So how will we children of God live our lives during our short stay on this earth? We know where to turn for the answer.

The Bible says, "Since we are surrounded by such a great cloud of witnesses, let us get rid of every burden and the sin that so easily ensnares us, and let us run with patient endurance the race that is laid out for us. Let us keep our eyes fixed on Jesus" (Hebrews 12:1,2).

Did you catch the tangle that tries to take us down? "The sin that so easily ensnares us." So many things can trip us up and take us away from God. Temptations lurk about. Sin slithers into every facet of this world. The devil dances with delight when our thoughts, words, and actions stray from Bible teachings. The Bible warns us, "Do not give the Devil an opportunity" (Ephesians 4:27).

We don't always think about the way we live our lives as having the potential to "give the Devil an opportunity" to wedge his way further into our existence. So many things seem so harmless. Whether it be a movie or TV show we watch; a book, website, or magazine we read; or a party we attend so often we don't realize their importance to our Christian living. We see them as just an escape, but Satan sees them as an occasion to steer us away from the truth. We start to attach meaning to meaningless things. Sin pollutes us and anxiety returns. The old evil foe once again takes control of our lives. Paul warned Timothy (and also us): "Guard what has been entrusted to you, turning away from godless, empty talk and the contraditions of what is falsely called 'knowledge.' By professing it, some have veered away from the faith" (1 Timothy 6:20,21).

Too often, the earthly things become our main focus and veer us away from the faith. This world, this life, becomes our home, and in the end, we lose sight on what is most important. We become so absorbed in the things of this world that we forget where our true home lies. We forget about our permanent place for eternity, our heavenly home. "If you call on the Father who judges impartially, according to the work of each person, conduct yourselves during the time of your pilgrimage in reverence" (1 Peter 1:17). During this pilgrimage, we often forget that we are, as Paul describes, "We are God's workmanship, created in Christ Jesus for good works, which God prepared in advance so that we would walk in them" (Ephesians 2:10).

This comes back to persevering in the faith again. James described it this way: "Let patient endurance finish its work, so that you may be mature and complete, not lacking anything" (James 1:4). It's not letting the sinful things of this world, and in the heavenly realms, derail us from our spiritual target. Instead we "press on toward the goal, for the prize of the upward call of God in Christ Jesus" (Philippians 3:14).

So how should we live our lives? Jesus said, "Remain in me, and I am going to remain in you" (John 15:4). This is where our focus needs to be—remaining connected to Jesus Christ and the truth of his Word. This means testing the things in this world to see if they are from God. "Test everything. Hold on to the good. Keep away from every kind of evil" (1 Thessalonians 5:21,22). Remaining connected to Jesus means to focusing our minds on the heavenly ideals. "Because you were raised with Christ, seek the things that are above, where Christ is seated at the right hand of God. Set your mind on things above, not on earthly things" (Colossians 3:1,2). Remaining connected to Jesus means thinking thoughts that line up with spiritual truths of our God. "Those who are in harmony with the sinful flesh think about things the way the sinful flesh does, and those in harmony with the spirit think about things the way the spirit does" (Romans 8:5).

I'm sure you are seeing that the Bible has numerous passages that direct us how to live our lives. You may be wondering, How does this relate to anxiety? Our anxiety comes from being apart from God, from not being connected to Jesus. Isaiah pointed out how peace comes through our connection to our Savior. "You preserve perfect peace for the person whose resolve is steadfast, because he trusts in you" (Isaiah 26:3). "Come near to God, and he will come near to you" (James 4:8).

We want to be close to God. We want to connect with and remain in Jesus Christ. The way we live our lives make a difference. Peter points this out. "For this very reason, after applying every effort, add moral excellence to your faith. To moral excellence, add knowledge. To knowledge, add self-control. To self-control, add patient endurance. To patient endurance, add godliness. To godliness, add brotherly affection. And to brotherly affection, add love. For if you have these qualities and they are increasing, they are going to keep you from being idle or unfruitful in regard to your knowledge of our Lord Jesus Christ" (2 Peter 1:5-8). So run the race marked out for you in a way that is pleasing to God. "Do you not know that when runners compete in the stadium, they all run, but only one receives the prize? Run like that—to win" (1 Corinthians 9:24).

Our time on this earth is almost up. "The night is almost over, and the day is drawing near. So let us put away the deeds of darkness and put on the weapons of light. Let us walk decently as in the daytime, not in carousing and drunkenness, not in sexual sin and wild living, not in strife and jealousy. Instead, clothe yourselves with the Lord Jesus Christ, and do not give any thought to satisfying the desires of your sinful flesh" (Romans 13:12-14). Let's live our lives connected to and clothed with Jesus.

TEN

Prayer

"At every opportunity, pray in the Spirit
with every kind of prayer and petition."
Ephesians 6:18

Prayer. Something so often neglected and forgotten. Something so important. Something our heavenly Father tells us to do continually. "Rejoice always. Pray without ceasing. In everything give thanks. For this is God's will for you in Christ Jesus" (1 Thessalonians 5:16-18). As we go through our day, there is no time or place where we cannot talk to God–anytime, any-place, always speaking to our heavenly Father.

Praying doesn't have to be something others notice. In contrast to those who wanted to be seen for their prayers, Jesus points people to private prayers.

"Whenever you pray, go into your private room, close your door, and pray to your Father who is unseen. And your Father, who sees what others cannot see, will reward you" (Matthew 6:6). Even if this "closing the door" is only in your mind, it is enough. You don't have to be on your knees as long as you are in your heart. You can be on a bus, on a plane, in a crowded room, walking, running, it doesn't matter. Others may never notice. Remember, "The Lord is near. Do not worry about anything, but in everything, by prayer and petition, with thanksgiving, let your requests be made known to God. And the peace of God, which surpasses all understanding, will guard your hearts and your minds in Christ Jesus" (Philippians 4:5-7).

In all my struggles with anxiety, God has always been faithful: always true to his Word, always near. I know the most important thing to do before any situation that may present anxious moments is to go to my God in prayer. So many times fear was there before the event then fear evaporated during the event; then fear may even have come during the event, and then it was gone. I asked for his help before, during, and after the event. And God helped. "I sought the LORD, and he answered me. From all my terrors he delivered me" (Psalm 34:4). I've seen the Lord answer. I've seen him deliver. I know where my help comes from. Psalms, the hymnbook of the Old Testament, sings of God's help given to the one who prays. "In my distress I called to the LORD. To my God I cried out. He heard my voice from his temple. My cry came before him. It reached his ears" (Psalm 18:6). "O LORD my God, I cried out to you, and you healed me" (Psalm 30:2). "I lift up my eyes to the mountains. Where does my help come from? My help comes from the LORD, the Maker of heaven and earth" (Psalm 121:1,2).

At times, we may not even know what to pray for. No need for concern. The Holy Spirit speaks for us. "In the same way the Spirit helps us in our weakness. We do not know what we should pray for, but the Spirit himself intercedes for us with groans that are not expressed in words. And he who searches our hearts knows what the mind of the Spirit is, because the Spirit intercedes for the saints, according to God's will" (Romans 8:26,27). God knows what we want and, more important, what we need even before we ask.

Prayer is important. The prophet Daniel knew the importance of prayer even when praying could cost him his life. Remember the story? King Darius was persuaded by those who sought Daniel's demise to issue a decree that prohibited "anyone to pray a prayer to any god or person for thirty days except to [King Darius]. Anyone who does so will be thrown into the den of lions" (Daniel 6:7). What did this do to Daniel? Silence him? Scare him? Stop him? Hardly. "When Daniel learned that the document had been signed, he went to his house. It had windows on its upper story that opened toward Jerusalem. Three times each day he would get on his knees and pray and offer praise before his God. He continued to do that, just as he had been doing before this" (Daniel 6:10). Prayer put him at odds with the law and led to his living with lions for an evening. But Daniel knew prayer was that important.

How did he come to know the importance of prayer? Because Daniel saw the power of God time and time again—friends spared from a fiery furnace, lion mouths muzzled, and dream interpretations delivered. Listen to Daniel's description of God's might: "'How can this servant of my lord speak with my lord? And I, from now on—no strength remains in me, and no breath is left in me.' The one whose appearance was like a man touched me again and strengthened me. He said to me, 'Do not be afraid, you highly valued man. Peace to you. Be strong! Be strong!' As he spoke with me I was strengthened, and I said, 'Keep speaking, my lord, because you strengthen me'" (Daniel 10:17-19).

"Do not be afraid." "Fear not." Abraham, Moses, Daniel, Mary, and many more biblical characters heard those words. We hear those words and know they are for us too. Be at ease; God is with us and answers the prayers of his people. He doesn't want us to be anxious or afraid. He rescues us from all our fears. He strengthens us when we are weak. Here's how we know: "Do you not know? Have you not heard? The LORD is the eternal God. He is the Creator of the ends of the earth. He will not grow tired, and he will not become weary. No one can find a limit to his understanding. He is the one who gives strength to the weak, and he increases the strength of those who lack power. Young men grow tired and become weary. Even strong men stumble and fall. But those who wait for the LORD will receive new strength. They will lift up their wings and soar like eagles. They will run and not become weary. They will walk and not become tired" (Isaiah 40:28-31). The Lord gives strength, increases strength, and delivers new strength.

The first Christians also knew the importance of prayer. They practiced it and put it as a priority. "They continued to hold firmly to the apostles' teaching and to the fellowship, to the breaking of the bread, and to the prayers" (Acts 2:42). The apostles themselves, when feeling distracted by the distribution of food, said, "We will put [the deacons, leaders within the church] in charge of this service. But we will devote ourselves to prayer and the ministry of the word" (Acts 6:3,4). Early believers knew the importance of prayer.

Prayers remind us of our close relationship to our Savior. Moses said, "What other great nation is there that has a god as close to it as the LORD our God is to us whenever we call on him?" (Deuteronomy 4:7). God listens to our prayers, and he answers our prayers. "Come, listen, all you who fear God, and let me tell what he has done to save my life. To him I cried out with my mouth. High praise was on my tongue. If I had contemplated evil in my heart, the Lord would not have listened, but God has surely listened. He has paid attention to the sound of my prayer. Blessed be God, who has not turned aside my prayer or turned aside his mercy from me!" (Psalm 66:16-20). His ever-hearing ears hear our every prayer.

But God doesn't only listen to our prayers; he always answers. "Call on me and I will answer you. I will show you great and mysterious things you did not know" (Jeremiah 33:3). It may not always be the answer we hope for, but it is always for our good.

No matter how anxious we may be, no matter how much anxiety is in our heart, our God can answer our need in the best way and go bigger than we could ever dream. Approach him in prayer. "Now to him, who is able, according to the power that is at work within us, to do infinitely more than we can ask or imagine, to him be the glory in the church and in Christ Jesus throughout all generations, forever and ever! Amen" (Ephesians 3:20,21).

ELEVEN

In Christ

"If anyone is in Christ, he is a new creation.
The old has passed away. The new has come!"
2 Corinthians 5:17

My last name is Woodington. I didn't choose that name. It was given to me. I am a Woodington because my father was a Woodington, and his father was a Woodington, etc. You say, "Tell me something I don't know." I am using this as an analogy. The analogy is that I am a sinner because my parents were sinners, and their parents were sinners, and their parents were sinners, etc., all the way back to the original sinner (Adam). I inherit what is of Adam (1 Corinthians 15:45,47). "As through the disobedience of one man the many became sinners" (Romans 5:19). I sin because I am a sinner. I am not a sinner because I sin. It is who I am. It comes naturally to me. I am the problem.

I am in Adam. Do you know what it means to be *in* someone? If your grandfather had died at the age of 3, where would you be? You would not be here. You would have died in him! You were in his loins, so to speak. Because I am in Adam, I receive everything that is of Adam.

If we are in Christ, however, we receive everything that is of Christ. "So also through the obedience of one man the many will become righteous" (Romans 5:19). How are we to get into Christ? The Bible tells us we are in Christ! God has done this for us. "Because of him you are in Christ Jesus" (1 Corinthians 1:30).

Do you know that you died? Bondage to sin comes by birth, deliverance from sin comes by death. Paul makes this point: "The love of Christ compels us, because we came to this conclusion: One died for all; therefore, all died" (2 Corinthians 5:14). When Jesus was crucified, all of us were crucified with him. This person. This person you struggle with every day . . .

is no more. "Do you not know that all of us who were baptized into Christ Jesus were baptized into his death?" (Romans 6:3). Your baptism connects you directly to Jesus' death.

When Christ died, you died. When Christ rose, you were given a new life. Go back to 1 Corinthians 15:45,47. Notice two remarkable terms used to describe Jesus. He is the *last Adam* and the *second man*. As the last Adam, Jesus is the sum total of all humanity. The cross put an end to this seemingly endless chain of Adams. When Jesus died on the cross, all that was of Adam was crucified. Jesus was crucified to the world and the world was crucified to him. All that was of the first Adam was done away in him. Because we are "in Christ," we died when Jesus died. Through our baptism we were there when he died on the cross.

God dealt with all our sins by the blood of Christ. God deals with us by the cross of Christ. If a city wanted to eliminate all alcohol, it could have representatives go door-to-door and confiscate all alcohol. Would that solve the problem? No, not as long as the factories keep making alcohol. The city would need to ensure all the factories are closed. This is what God did. He closed the sin factory. When Jesus died on the cross, he eliminated our sin factory bodies! "We died to sin" (Romans 6:2).

Jesus is also referred to as the *second man.* As the second man he is the head of a new group of people with a new life. The union with him begins in his resurrection and lasts into eternity, which never ends. "We were therefore buried with him by this baptism into his death, so that just as he was raised from the dead through the glory of the Father, we too would also walk in a new life" (Romans 6:4). When Jesus rose, we rose! So closely does our baptism connect us to Jesus that his resurrection to life means we rose also to a new life. Child of God. Christian. Saint. Believer. Citizen of heaven. We have a new life in Christ that will never end. The apostle Paul reminds us, "If we have been united with him in the likeness of his death, we will certainly also be united with him in the likeness of his resurrection" (Romans 6:5). We died in him as the last Adam; we live in him as the second man. Paul also stated, "I have been crucified with Christ, and I no longer live, but Christ lives in me. The life I am now living in the flesh, I live by faith in the Son of God, who loved me and gave himself for me" (Galatians 2:20).

But what about the sins you committed an hour ago, yesterday, last week, last month? And you keep on failing and plunging headfirst into sins. That's the dead person. You have a new life in Christ! By the Spirit's grace you are now "in Christ." Daily drown the dead person, the Old Adam, in the waters of your baptism. The new person the Holy Spirt brings to life through gospel promises says "no" to sin and "yes" to Christ and Christian living. That's who you are. That's your identity as one who is "in Christ."

When anxiety overwhelms, don't look at what you see in your failures and sins. Listen to what God states about your identity: You are in Christ. When worries seem to wind their way around every fiber of your being, don't get tangled up in the trap of no hope. Take to heart God's promises about what he has made you to be: You are in Christ. When your nerves are fried and frayed, don't zero in on that which consumes you. Concentrate your attention on what has a zero chance of failing because of God's actions through Jesus: You are in Christ. That's your true identity.

One man who could have been sickened with a sore case of overwhelming anxiety knew his true identity. His name was Lazarus. A successful rich man, however, lost his identity in his worldly wealth:

There was a rich man who was dressed in purple and fine linen, living in luxury every day. A beggar named Lazarus had been laid at his gate. Lazarus was covered with sores and longed to be fed with what fell from the rich man's table. Besides this, the dogs also came and licked his sores. Eventually the beggar died, and the angels carried him to Abraham's side. The rich man also died and was buried. In hell, where he was in torment, he lifted up his eyes and saw Abraham far away and Lazarus at his side. He called out and said, "Father Abraham, have mercy on me! Send Lazarus to dip the tip of his finger in water and cool my tongue, because I am in misery in this flame."

But Abraham said, "Son, remember that in your lifetime you received your good things, and Lazarus received bad things. But now he is comforted here, and you are in misery. Besides all this, a great chasm has been set in place between us and you, so that those who want to cross from here to you cannot, nor can anyone cross over from there to us."

He said, "Then I beg you, father, send him to my father's home, because I have five brothers—to warn them, so that they will not also come to this place of torment."

Abraham said, "They have Moses and the Prophets. Let them listen to them."

"No, father Abraham," he said, "but if someone from the dead goes to them, they will repent."

Abraham replied to him, "If they do not listen to Moses and the Prophets, they will not be convinced even if someone rises from the dead." (Luke 16:19-31)

Earthly riches consumed the rich man's heart, and in turn, consumed his identity. He lost everything in the consuming fires of hell. Through God's promises of the Savior, Lazarus knew his true identity on earth and in his eternal heavenly home. He was in Christ.

Through faith in Jesus, you are "in Christ." This is your identity. If you lose everything in this life, you've lost nothing. You are a new creation. Christ's perfect life is your life. Christ's death is your death. Christ's resurrected life is your new life. You are in Christ.

Conclusion

"As for you, continue in the things you have learned
and about which you have become convinced.
You know from whom you learned them."
2 Timothy 3:14

In this book, I have tried to share with you what I have become convinced of. I am not a psychologist or psychiatrist, but I believe God has used my struggle with anxiety to discipline me, teach me, and draw me to him. He has used this to help me turn away from trusting in myself. He has used this to teach me the truth found only in his Word. He has used this to help me trust in him. An imprisoned apostle Paul wrote, "That is why I am suffering these things. But I am not ashamed, because I know the one in whom I have believed, and I am convinced that he is able to guard what I have entrusted to him until that day"

(2 Timothy 1:12). And what have I entrusted to him? My faith.

My struggle goes on. As long as I live on this earth, I will have to recite right alongside Paul, "I know that good does not live in me, that is, in my sinful flesh. The desire to do good is present with me, but I am not able to carry it out. So I fail to do the good I want to do. Instead, the evil I do not want to do, that is what I keep doing. Now if I do what I do not want to do, it is no longer I who am doing it, but it is sin living in me" (Romans 7:18-20). But I don't stop there. I also have to recite something else Paul wrote a few verses later: "What a miserable wretch I am! Who will rescue me from this body of death? I thank God through Jesus Christ our Lord!" (Romans 7:24,25). You see, this struggle between the old man and the new man . . . this struggle will be there in each of us until the day we die. But through the gospel in the Word and sacraments, the new man continues to become stronger. Stronger for the battle. Stronger to live in faith.

Focus on a key word Paul used in the Romans passage: *rescue*. Do you see the power and comfort in that word? Jesus rescues. He's the one who made the heroic act of pulling us out of the burning fire of hell. When sin consumed us, Jesus pulled us to safety. When the devil doused us with the gasoline of guilt and lit the match, Jesus washed us in our baptismal waters and forgave us. That's a rescue. That's a rescuer who knows what we need. "Let us approach the throne of grace with confidence, so that we may receive mercy and find grace to help in time of need" (Hebrews 4:16). You will see this mercy and grace time and again in your life. Look for it. Watch for it. Jesus rescues.

When you experience anxiety, remember the way out is always the same. *Facing it*—not running away. Remember God's promise, "No temptation has overtaken you except what is common to mankind. And God is faithful; he will not let you be tempted beyond what you can bear. But when you are tempted, he will also provide a way out so that you can endure it" (1 Corinthians 10:13). Encouraging words from our

God: You are able to bear it. The way out of anxiety is *accepting it*—view your experience as a positive one. With certainty you can know that God will work it for your good. An apostle who had experienced numerous events in his life that could leave him dealing with anxiety wrote, "We know that all things work together for the good of those who love God, for those who are called according to his purpose" (Romans 8:28). The way out of anxiety is *understanding discipline.* God disciplines us out of pure love as his own dear children. "No discipline seems pleasant when it is happening, but painful, yet later it yields a peaceful harvest of righteousness for those who have been trained by it" (Hebrews 12:11). God brings blessings out of discipline. Remember that your Savior went to the darkest depths of hell's dungeon to rescue you from your sinful situation. When it comes to anxiety, return to that loving action of your God. And then face, accept, and understand this anxiety and discipline for what it is. Trust your Savior who keeps every one of his promises.

My anxiety is my thorn, my hardship, my weakness. And I rejoice in this, just like the apostle Paul: "I will be glad to boast all the more in my weaknesses, so that the power of Christ may shelter me. That is why I delight in weaknesses, in insults, in hardships, in persecutions, in difficulties, for the sake of Christ. For whenever I am weak, then am I strong" (2 Corinthians 12:9,10). "*Then* am I *strong*!" What power. Christ's power! Christ's strength is in me in the midst of weakness. Christ's power shelters me in my hardship. Christ's might brings a perseverance that matures my faith. James, the half-brother of Jesus, understood this well. "Consider it complete joy, my brothers, whenever you fall into various kinds of trials, because you know that the testing of your faith produces patient endurance. And let patient endurance finish its work, so that you may be mature and complete, not lacking anything" (James 1:2-4).

Accept your anxiety. Rejoice in your sufferings. Roman Christians heard the same message, "We also rejoice confidently in our sufferings, because we know that suffering produces patient endurance, and patient endurance produces tested character, and tested character produces hope. And hope will not put us to shame, because God's love has been poured out into our hearts by the Holy Spirit, who was given to us" (Romans 5:3-5). God takes the anxiety you experience and uses it to develop you as his Christian child. He shapes you, builds you, loves you, and equips you by his Spirit so he can lead you into having hope, biblical hope. That's hope that anticipates what's coming. It's hope that looks and longs and can't wait until what was promised arrives. And what is this hope? Our hope is eternal life. It's the life we have waiting for us where anxiety, suffering, and weakness are nowhere to be found.

All this accepting anxiety, celebrating in suffering, or persevering through pressures can only happen when we are standing on our foundation. That foundation is the assurance of eternity in heaven through our God who "so loved the world that he gave his only-begotten Son, that whoever believes in him shall not perish, but have eternal life" (John 3:16). What truly matters is knowing Jesus Christ is our ruler and rescuer. It's knowing that his death on the cross delivered the costly payment to free us from our sins. His resurrection gives us a new life here and into eternity. And it's already done. The victory is complete. Heaven awaits us!

So, my dear friends, my rescued-and-delivered-from-death friends, it's good to return to words we heard before. They're words that get us battle-ready for every evil attack that would attempt to shake and destroy our foundation:

Finally, be strong in the Lord and in his mighty power. Put on the full armor of God, so that you can stand against the schemes of the Devil. For our struggle is not against flesh and blood, but against the rulers, against the authorities, against the world rulers of this darkness, against the spiritual forces of evil in the heavenly places. For this reason, take up the full armor of God, so that you will be able to take a stand on the evil day and, after you have done everything, to stand. Stand, then, with the belt of truth buckled around your waist, with the breastplate of righteousness fastened in place, and with the readiness that comes from the gospel of peace tied to your feet like sandals. At all times hold up the shield of faith, with which you will be able to extinguish all the flaming arrows of the Evil One. Also take the helmet of salvation and the sword of the Spirit, which is the word of God. At every opportunity, pray in the Spirit with every kind of prayer and petition. Stay alert for the same reason, always persevering in your intercession for all the saints. (Ephesians 6:10-18)

And never forget the following Bible passages that give great comfort in times of anxiety and stress. Let them dwell in your heart:

- "Consider it complete joy, my brothers, whenever you fall into various kinds of trials, because you know that the testing of your faith produces patient endurance. And let patient endurance finish its work, so that you may be mature and complete, not lacking anything." (James 1:2-4)

- "I will be glad to boast all the more in my weaknesses, so that the power of Christ may shelter me. That is why I delight in weaknesses, in insults, in hardships, in persecutions, in difficulties, for the sake of Christ. For whenever I am weak, then am I strong." (2 Corinthians 12:9,10)

- "No temptation has overtaken you except what is common to mankind. And God is faithful; he will not let you be tempted beyond what you can bear. But when you are tempted, he will also provide a way out so that you can endure it." (1 Corinthians 10:13)

- "I have said to you, "You are my servant." I have chosen you and not rejected you. Do not fear, for I am with you. Do not be overwhelmed, for I am your God. I will strengthen you. Yes, I will help you. I will uphold you with my righteous right hand." (Isaiah 41:9,10)

- "I have been crucified with Christ, and I no longer live, but Christ lives in me." (Galatians 2:20)